Improvement in 3-D

Book 1

DELEGATION
The Art of Letting Go!
Workbook

Delegation

Amy K. Atcha

Improvement in 3-D

Book 1

DELEGATION
The Art of Letting Go!
Workbook

Delegation

Delegation: The Art of Letting Go! Workbook
By: Amy K. Atcha

Copyright 2014 Customized Caring, Inc.

Cover design by: Wayne Johnson

Published by: Customized Caring Publishing
ISBN – 13: 978-0692215968

For information about special discounts on bulk purchases,
Contact Customized Caring, Inc. at 630.306.4480 or www.customizedcaring.com.

Delegation

About this Book

The Delegation: The Art of Letting Go! workbook is part of the Improvement in 3-D series. It has been designed to provide you with the opportunity to absorb the concepts, acquire the skills and advance your techniques, taking an active role in creating your leadership style. With Improvement in 3-D, you will learn, grow, and enhance your own delegation, due diligence and decision making abilities, as well as assisting those around you. As you study and strengthen your own skills, you will become more creative, more productive and more successful!

As a person, a group member, and as a leader, the information and questions in these books are designed to get you thinking. The exercises are designed to help you practice and implement new methods, expanding your gallery of techniques in all kinds of ways - personally, professionally, in your family, your work or any organization. You will be amazed as you watch your own skills grow to new heights, right along with those around you. Your attitude and style as a leader will never be the same.

The Improvement in 3-D workbooks are effective tools for learning, assessing, strategizing, and practicing methods and techniques. You can use these books for individual training and development, or with a group, to increase your productivity.

The information, tools and tips in these books will stay with you (and your organization) long after you finish the series. Use the guidance, structures and approaches over and over.

Are you ready to start? It's time for Improvement in 3-D!

Delegation

The Art of Letting Go!
Workbook

Contents

Delegation

Preface

Whether it's your first day on the job, your 20th year of helping out an organization, or you just need a bit more personal development in your life, it's never too soon (or too often!) for Improvement.

Improvement comes in many forms – mental, physical, structural and systematic – just to name a few. It can be achieved individually, in a group, and even as an organization. The great learners and scholars, along with entrepreneurs and businesspeople, never stop improving on themselves, their products, their thinking and their companies.

With each step that you take, you will grow, and seek out even more ways to improve. Soon, you will conceptualize, then visualize, strategize and formulate, and finally implement ways for Improvement.

The first of this three part series on Improvement is on Delegation. It is by no means the beginning of improvement, but it will help get you thinking, planning and working in a more productive and successful way.

As Andrew Carnegie said, "No man will make a great leader who wants to do it all himself or get all the credit for doing it."

Whether you are an experienced director or a newly christened trailblazer, you can take this one step further following John C. Maxwell's advice: "A leader is one who knows the way, goes the way and shows the way."

Thinking in 3-D conjures up many images — many dimensions — of the same, yet different, perspectives. When we think 3-D, we create a structure in our minds that references length, width and depth. In terms of working and creating, we may operate in 3-D:

> 1-D: doing it your way

> 2-D: asking others how they do it

> **3-D: working together to create a GREAT process, a GREAT product, a GREAT team**

The same goes for our Delegation, our Due Diligence and our Decision Making.

> Delegation — up, down and across

> Due Diligence from a variety of sources

> Decision Making, not just at one level, but considering other factors includes resources (time, money, people), style and method.

Throughout your work in this Improvement in 3-D Series, practice thinking in all three capacities, work on different levels and with different perspectives, and build on your success through knowledge, training and result!

The sections of this book will provide you with basic information and guidance about the concept and reasoning behind delegation, as well as the steps and instructions for some of the best approaches to delegation. At the back are Tools you can use to begin (or enhance) your Delegation skills.

LET GO! gives you the context in which we will use Delegation for this book.

Breaking It Down describes the What, Why, Who and How behind the technique of Delegation. It takes you step by step through the various aspects of the process, including providing you useful techniques and exercises.

Mastering the Art lets you practice the skills by trying out the techniques with simulations and scenarios.

Helpful Tools are resources provided for future study, practice and use.

It's time to LET GO! is your call to action!

Now is the time to absorb the knowledge.

Now is the time to enhance your abilities.

Now is the time to leverage your leadership potential.

Now is the time for Improvement in 3-D!

Delegation

LET GO!

Delegation has been defined in several ways, the majority of which state that it is the act of entrusting another person with a given responsibility, along with empowering that person with the authority to act. Delegation is a core concept of leadership.

In most instances, the Delegator (the person who had the original obligation) will retain the overall responsibility to ensure that the project/task is completed. However, that individual does not necessarily have to "do" all of the underlying tasks in order to render it a success.

Key to the process of delegation is the empowerment of authority to the delegatee. Without proper empowerment, the newly assigned may not have the appropriate powers to execute needed actions. Likewise, other persons involved will not know that this person has been given the duty to complete that specific task.

In the process of delegating a job to another and granting authority (empowering), the delegator must also 'remove' himself/herself from the minutiae of the task. This is not to say that the delegator should completely divest himself/herself from the on-goings of the project and/or its successful completion. However, once a project has been delegated, the Delegator must resist being overly involved, for fear of "micro-managing".

The purpose behind delegation (albeit usually several) is to lessen the involvement of the Delegator in the actual detailed workings of the task – whether it be for reasons of time, resource management, professional development, or otherwise. (We will discuss the various benefits for delegation later in the book.)

Delegation as a leadership principle is important for 1) efficiency and 2) development. Delegation is one of the most important management skills for leaders. The benefits are vast, for the leader, for the staff, and for the organization.

Delegation allows for the ability to use the best people for each portion of a particular job, thus creating efficiencies. The more expertise an individual has, the less resources it will take to accomplish a task.   This great leadership technique permits more people (employees, teams, etc.) to be actively involved.   It provides for the distribution of workload, while also motivating team members / employees by giving them value and importance.   Delegation can help you, your team, and your organization run more efficiently and productively.

Through leadership and delegation, you can provide (and receive) professional development and personal growth, a better appreciation of and use of time, and the engagement of more employees in an ever changing workforce.

To gain the most out of a delegation experience, YOU must know, personally, what you aim to obtain or achieve out of the arrangement. By having a personal and/or professional goal attached to each delegation assignment, you will have "skin in the game", be committed to the project, AND personally benefit.

Delegation is a tool that leaders (and managers) use for a variety of reasons. The key to successful delegation, however, is that it is done purposefully, and with a goal in mind. Simply shrugging off responsibility onto another person, and merely "walking away" is not delegation. With proper delegation, a leader will "LET GO" while still remaining involved in the process as well as the outcome of the project at hand.

Since LETting GO can mean different things to different people, let's start with a brief discussion and exercise about the components in   L E T   G O.

Leadership

Leadership has many characteristics. We tend to think of Leaders as managers, bosses or superiors. However, that's not the only means. Thinking more broadly, leadership can exist as positional, technical, mentoring, advisory, etc.

When I think of leadership, I think of:

1.

2.

3.

Leadership through Delegation means:

1.

2.

3.

Empowerment

Empowerment is the granting of authority to another person. This action can be communicated in a variety of ways, and with many associated dynamics and meanings.

When I think of empowerment, I think of:

1.

2.

3.

Ways I can empower my Delegatee:

1.

2.

3.

Training/Teaching

Teaching and training are involved with new hires, professional development and succession planning. Training never ends!

When I think of training, I think of:

1.

2.

3.

Areas of training provided through Delegation:

1.

2.

3.

Goal Oriented

Goals are the outcomes we want or expect from a given assignment, task or project. Goals can be personal or professional, tangible or intangible, specific or general. Thinking broadly, goals can include something as simple as "gaining greater, more varied experiences".

When I think of a project being goal oriented, I think of:

1.

2.

3.

Goals to be gained from Delegation include:

1.

2.

3.

Opportunity

Opportunity opens doors. Opportunity increases knowledge, exposure and experience. Opportunity is what we are all seeking – as a Delegator and a Delegatee.

When I think of Opportunity, I think of:

1.

2.

3.

Opportunities to be gained from Delegation include:

1.

2.

3.

For each project that is Delegated – both the Delegator and the Delegatee will be able to experience the assignment from the LET GO! perspective.

Let's practice. Consider one project - the assignment of a Month End Report to a subordinate. What is the benefit in each element for both the Delegator and the Delegatee? Do the benefits align? Fill in the blanks, then discuss.

Delegator   Delegatee

Leadership

_____   _____

Empowerment

_____   _____

Training

_____   _____

Goal Oriented

_____   _____

Opportunity

_____   _____

BIG NOTE HERE: We are talking about Delegation as a process to LET GO of control, LET GO of all the work, LET GO of insecurity and resistance.

We are learning to LET GO....

NOT to WALK AWAY!

As you will learn, through delegation, you are transferring some responsibility, the bulk of the work, and the perhaps even the power. However, YOU may still be ultimately accountable and answerable for the people, the process and the product. You are letting go of the details, but you are NOT walking away from the obligation of oversight.

Delegation

Breaking It Down

In this section, we will work on breaking down the Delegation model. We will discuss **What** to delegate and **Why?**, the **Advantages** and **Barriers** of delegation, **How** to delegate and to **Who**. We will end the chapter with a short discussion of the **Keys to Success**.

<u>What to Delegate and Why?</u>

Whether it's a repetitive task, a minor decision or simply helping another employee "grow", there are plenty of projects that can be delegated. Many assignments are made based upon the need to free up your own to-do list and/or share the workload among peers.

On the flip side, there are some duties that should NOT be delegated. These generally fall into the category of "personal" – matters requiring confidentiality, performance reviews, items specifically designated to be done by you, tasks you would not want others to do. Similarly, you would not want to delegate to someone who does not have the necessary qualification or designations, if that is significant to the task (don't designate to a young child work that needs to be done by a licensed professional). Not every job is appropriate for delegation.

There are many projects in which only a portion may be appropriate for delegation. That's fine too! The more help the better.

Think through your own personal and professional life. What matters have been delegated to you to do? Think broadly.....spouses delegate (or divide up) household chores among themselves, parents delegate to children, committees delegate responsibilities to each member. Get your creative mind working on what is *possible.*

Every good leader takes action only after having carefully thought through the possibilities and identified WHY actions, assignments, etc. should take place. The same is true with Delegation. The reasons why a particular project is delegated can vary extensively – from personal, to professional, to organizational. When considering an assignment to delegate, always identify Why it is being delegated. (Later we will discuss Why a particular Delegatee is selected). Your reasons may be many! Remember, in LETting GO – you must be Goal Oriented!

You may use a simple What and Why structure such as:

Assignment: _____

Part of the _____ Project

Reason(s) for Delegation:

    1) _____

    2) _____

    3) _____

Let's discuss…

What projects or tasks are appropriate for delegation?

1.

2.

3.

Reasons <u>why</u> to delegate include:

1.

2.

3.

What projects or tasks are <u>NOT</u> appropriate to delegate?

1.

2.

3.

Reasons why these projects should <u>NOT</u> be delegated:

1.

2.

3.

Advantages of Delegation

The reasons why delegation is important and appropriate lead right into its advantages. Delegation should be advantageous to the delegator, the delegatee, and to the organization as a whole. The benefits may be personal in nature, on a professional level or both!

The <u>Personal</u> BENEFITS I will gain from Delegating are:

1.

2.

3.

The <u>Professional</u> BENEFITS I will gain from Delegating are:

1.

2.

3.

The <u>Professional</u> BENEFITS my organization will gain from Delegating are:

1.

2.

3.

The <u>Personal</u> BENEFITS the Delegatee will gain are:

1.

2.

3.

The <u>Professional</u> BENEFITS the Delegatee will gain are:

1.

2.

3.

You can add to your simple What and Why structure with:

Assignment: _____

Part of the _____ Project

Benefit(s) to Delegator: _____

_____

Benefit(s) to Delegatee: _____

_____

Benefit(s) to Organization: _____

Five Steps to Delegation

There are five basic steps to delegation. While these are listed in order, that does prohibit you from revisiting and revising each step along the way. As circumstances change and your project develops, it may be necessary (and advantageous!) to work through the steps again, re-prioritizing and even re-assigning tasks.   Remember, Delegation is an art – and a very fluid one at that.

1. Prioritize

Identify the project(s) that you are going to delegate. These projects may be smaller pieces of a big project or simply one stand-alone assignment. If there is more than one project (or piece), rank the parts in order of priority. Priority might be based on time constraints, or process-flow ("A" must be finished before "B" can be started), or availability of personnel and resources.

Other possible ways to prioritize:

1.

2.

3.

2. Match project needs to <u>ability</u> and <u>availability</u> of each candidate

- Knowledge
- Motivation
- Availability

Now that you know WHAT will be delegated, spend some time thinking about the skills and knowledge that are needed to complete the task. Most commonly, we think in terms of computer skills, writing ability, communication talents, technical expertise, etc.

What other skills and knowledge might be important?

1.

2.

3.

Motivation is a very subjective term when it comes to delegation. Some individuals are motivated based on the desire to do well at a task; others are motivated by the opportunity to learn. Still others are motivated on nothing more than their current paycheck.

But why is motivation important? The level of motivation of the Delegatee may be directly related to the amount of time and energy you, as the Delegator, will need to expend to get the job done. Generally speaking, the MORE motivated the employee, the LESS influence (and muscle) you will need to show to get results.

Consider, for the particular assignment, and for the specific delegatee, what level of motivation will be required?

Finally, the availability of a candidate may be of concern. Depending on the task being assigned, its anticipated time commitment and selected due date, one or more individuals may not be available. Consider the level of urgency of the assignment. Will it be possible to have assignments of others, including your preferred candidate, shuffled (re-assigned, re-prioritized) to fit the need of this current project?

Is your brain swirling? Are you being creative? Are you thinking of ALL of your possibilities – even people you have not worked with before? Are you considering technical ability along with soft skills (interpersonal relations), work ethic, and vacation time?

As you weigh your options, identify several people who may be appropriate for the delegation assignment.

Leaders do not always "dictate" assignments, although sometimes that method is the best. There are alternative ways to obtain willing Delegatees. You may even decide to ask for volunteers for a particular assignment. If this is the case, be sure to rank each fairly and honestly. Just because someone WANTS to work on a project, might not mean that he/she is well suited for that project.

Other possible ways to find candidates:

1.

2.

3.

Next, rank each candidate in terms of the knowledge they already possess related to the assignment, their motivation as a "team player" or employee (if this is applicable), and their ability to work on the project at this time (do he/she have other high priority assignments?). Your ranking criteria can be in whatever method you choose (scale of 1-10, order 1-3, etc.), and can even vary from one category to another, as long as it is consistent for all candidates.

Other possible ways to rank candidates:

1.

2.

3.

You may find it helpful to use a chart to summarize your deliberations.

Project: _____

Name	Knowledge	Motivation	Availability	Total

3. Assign responsibility / empower/ grant authority

- **Describe task and expectations**
- **Identify training needs**
- **Identify resources**

You know WHAT you want to delegate, and WHO you want to delegate to. Now it's time to actually do it! It's time to DELEGATE!

Before you call your latest selection in to surprise him/her with their new assignment, let's stop to consider what exactly you will tell them. What specifically do you want the delegatee to do? What expectations do you have of the person, and the progress and the result? Does that person need any training prior to beginning the assignment? Does he/she need any additional resources (computer programs, additional helpers, money, supplies) to perform effectively and efficiently?

Think first, speak second.

How would you describe the task you are assigning? There are many ways: summary form, step by step instructions, output/outcome desired, etc. Be sure the responsibility, time requirements (if any), and process are clear and detailed.

In what manner would you describe the task? What other ways are acceptable? When do methods differ?

1.

2.

3.

What are your expectations with respect to the Person, the Process (the manner in which the assignment is completed), and the Result?

Person

1.

2.

3.

Process

1.

2.

3.

Result

1.

2.

3.

With respect to both training and resources, your aim should be to provide the most and best possible. Unfortunately, your own budget (time and money) may render this impossible. Consider your possibilities and select which skills training and resources will best fit your need, while also being consistent with your financial and operational plans.

What types of training are required for best performance?

1.

2.

3.

What resources are needed for success?

1.

2.

3.

With the project assigned and resources provided, you (and the Delegatee) may find the attention, cooperation and respect of others is needed to best work the assignment and complete the task. You, as the Delegator, will need to "Empower" your Delegatee.

Empowerment of a Delegatee may be as simple as sending out an e-mail to the respective staff informing them of the project, the Delegatee's role, and a request for cooperation. In other instances, in order for the Delegatee to perform, you may need to grant that person specific access to computer programs, databases or authority to communicate (and direct) others.

What other areas might empowerment / access be needed by the Delegatee?

1.

2.

3.

One typical method in which a Delegatee is granted authority is via written communication – either e-mail or memorandum. However, this is certainly not the only manner.

What other methods might a Delegatee become empowered?

1.

2.

3.

4. Monitor and Encourage (continued accountability)

You've made your selection and delegated the project tasks. However, your job is not over yet! You must continue to monitor your Delegatees, encouraging them (if necessary) until the project is completed.

The best method of monitoring is through periodic status meetings with reports, although this is not the only method.

What other ways can you monitor the person and the progress of the assigned task?

1.

2.

3.

Encouragement may also be necessary, especially if the assignment is new for the Delegatee, or if the Delegatee lacks confidence. At times, a simple "Good job" or "Keep it up!" may be enough. These are only a few suggestions.

What other ways might you encourage a Delegatee?

1.

2.

3.

5. Evaluate

Let's not forget to evaluate. Evaluation most certainly should be done at the end of the assignment, but should also be conducted throughout the course of the project (this leads back to the monitoring function).

Likewise, evaluations can be performed not only by the Delegator of the Delegatee, but also by the Delegatee of the Delegator, and even by an outsider for both parties.

As you recall, delegation can be a benefit to both the Delegator and the Delegatee. As such, it's in the best interest of each person to conduct self-evaluations, as well as evaluations on each other.

When evaluating others, it is important to let the evaluatee know what they have been doing well (so they keep doing it!) as much as to identify areas where improvement is needed (and bluntly, things to stop doing).

For successful evaluations, be fair, honest and specific. Remember, your objective in an evaluation is to have the Evaluatee understand their strengths, learn from their weaknesses, and feel as if they have been fairly, professionally, and respectfully reviewed.

A basic format for an evaluation is as follows. Use the format below to practice giving an evaluation.

Areas of Strength (positives)

1.

2.

3.

Areas Needing Improvement (negatives)

1.

2.

3.

Overall view/ opinion

_____

_____

_____

_____

What are the barriers to delegation?

No delegation assignment will come free of barriers – either by Delegator, the Delegatee or both. We carry with us our own "insecurities", as well as real, operational constraints. It's important to identify our barriers, both personal and professional, so that we can consider the impact each may have on a delegation assignment.

My Personal BARRIERS to Delegating are:

1.

2.

3.

Professional BARRIERS I (or my organization) have to Delegating are:

1.

2.

3.

Who can I delegate to?

We tend to think of delegation occurring only in a downward direction – Boss to Employee, Supervisor to Subordinate. While this is typically the case, it's important to remember that we may also be in situation where it is appropriate to delegate across (Peer to Peer) and even delegate UP (Employee to Boss).   There may even be instances where delegation can occur across departments or divisions.

Each delegation experience will vary depending on the nature of the project, the specific personnel and the dynamics of an organization. Think broadly! Be creative!

I <u>MAY</u> be able to delegate to:

Employees / subordinates:

1.

2.

3.

Peers:

1.

2.

3.

Supervisors / Superiors

1.

2.

3.

Others outside my department / division

1.

2.

3.

Keys to Success

Purpose

To achieve the greatest rewards and have the most positive experiences (i.e. SUCCESS), it is essential to have AND know the purpose behind what and why you are delegating. It is just as essential that your Delegatee know why and how the assignment will benefit him/her and/or the organization. As you work through your project delegation plan (yes, you should PLAN prior to just assigning), make a note as to the purpose and perceived benefits to each party for the delegation assignment.

Communication

As with all matters big and small, communication is key. The method as well as the manner in which instruction, evaluation, encouragement, and yes, even discipline, is given can make or break the motivation and success of the project. Keep RESPECT at the forefront of any exchanges – written or verbal, individual or group based.

Motivation

Knowing your values, your goals, and what makes you (and your team) excited and eager about a project or task, will keep both you and the project on the track to success. Find out what motivates each person – Delegator and Delegatee – and strive to posit assignments, encouragement and evaluation with this in mind.

Patience

We all need to have patience, whether its at home or at work. Remember, Delegation is an ART. You will not have a "perfect" experience your first time, your second time, or maybe ever. The key to remember is to learn along the way, and work to improve and enhance your skills through your experiences. For this, you need Patience.

Delegation

Mastering the Art

We've talked about Delegation – how and why to LET GO, and even broken it down step by step. Now, let's practice.

Following are 3 scenarios. After reading the summary of each, fill in the worksheet that follows.

Scenario One: Jack and Jill

On a monthly basis, Jill is required to issue a Contact report to the directors of her company, Marketing Madness, Inc., detailing the number, type and success of the promotion efforts of her department. Although each of her 5 employees keeps track of their own statistics, it is necessary for Jill to compile the data, sending only one spreadsheet, with a cover report to each director. The reports are due out (issued in hard copy) by the 5th working day of each month, capturing and reporting data from the previous month.

Statistics captured must include: date of contact, method of contact (phone, e-mail, in person, other), success (did contact result in promotional material request), date promotional material request was made of Mailing department.

Promotional materials are sent by the Mailing department only after being requisitioned with the appropriate form.

Scenario Two: The Protocols Project

Janet is responsible for ensuring that all Office Policy and Protocol documentation for the company is current, organized and available both electronically and in hard copy. Although she initially maintained the files herself, her job duties have increased not leaving sufficient time to accomplish all tasks effectively.

Office policies and protocols include General office business, Sales, Inventory and Customer Service. Janet has no employees that report directly to her, although she has been told she may request assistance from others as appropriate. Janet is used to working alone, so she is hesitant to ask for help.

Access to the electronic files for the protocols is limited to Janet, and her boss Bob. There are no exceptions to this rule.

Scenario Three: National Conference

The Skyscraper National Conference is held every year in February. Venues are secured at least 2 years in advance, with the upcoming conference to be held at the Columbia Center in Seattle. At present, no further arrangements have been made. William is responsible for the 3-day meeting for the upcoming year, after having helped his boss Jonathon last year at the Houston conference.

William works in the Event Planning department with 2 other people. As Chairperson this year, he will be responsible for a professional, yet creative event, and may even receive a bonus if successful.

Conference planning includes catering, guest speakers, formal banquet & awards night, hotel logistics, technology set up, hospitality packets, and networking events.

In past years, the conference has been attended by a variety of businesses representing market sectors of hotel, condominium housing, restaurants, small and large businesses, engineering and maintenance, and sales and promotion.

SCENARIO ONE: Jack and Jill

Name of Project: _____

Who is the Delegator: _____

Tasks:

Task	Why?	Time required	Due Date	Priority

Benefits to:
    Delegator   Delegatee

Barriers to:
    Delegator   Delegatee

Possible Personnel:

Name	Knowledge	Motivation	Availability	Total

Who was selected as the Delegatee?   Why?

How should the assignment be communicated to the Delegatee?

What are the expectations of the Delegator?

What are the expectations of the Delegatee?

How should the Delegator grant authority to the Delegatee? Do others need to be informed?

What Resources are needed by the Delegatee?

What training / teaching is involved?

What are the goals of the Delegator?

What are the goals of the Delegatee?

What opportunities exist for the Delegator?

What opportunities exist for the Delegatee?

How, and how often should the Delegatee be monitored?

How, and how often should the Delegatee be encouraged/ motivated?

Who should be evaluated? How often? By whom?

What problems could arise that would cause the Delegator to need extra patience?

What problems might arise that would cause the Delegatee to need extra patience?

<u>SCENARIO TWO: The Protocols Project</u>

Name of Project: _____

Who is the Delegator: _____

Tasks:

Task	Why?	Time required	Due Date	Priority

Benefits to:
   Delegator   Delegatee

Barriers to:
   Delegator   Delegatee

Possible Personnel:

Name	Knowledge	Motivation	Availability	Total

Who was selected as the Delegatee?   Why?

How should the assignment be communicated to the Delegatee?

What are the expectations of the Delegator?

What are the expectations of the Delegatee?

How should the Delegator grant authority to the Delegatee? Do others need to be informed?

What Resources are needed by the Delegatee?

What training / teaching is involved?

What are the goals of the Delegator?

What are the goals of the Delegatee?

What opportunities exist for the Delegator?

What opportunities exist for the Delegatee?

How, and how often should the Delegatee be monitored?

How, and how often should the Delegatee be encouraged/ motivated?

Who should be evaluated?   How often? By whom?

What problems could arise that would cause the Delegator to need extra patience?

What problems might arise that would cause the Delegatee to need extra patience?

SCENARIO THREE: National Conference

Name of Project: _____

Who is the Delegator: _____

Tasks:

Task	Why?	Time required	Due Date	Priority

Benefits to:
        Delegator   Delegatee

Barriers to:
        Delegator   Delegatee

Possible Personnel:

Name	Knowledge	Motivation	Availability	Total

Who was selected as the Delegatee?   Why?

How should the assignment be communicated to the Delegatee?

What are the expectations of the Delegator?

What are the expectations of the Delegatee?

How should the Delegator grant authority to the Delegatee? Do others need to be informed?

What Resources are needed by the Delegatee?

What training / teaching is involved?

What are the goals of the Delegator?

What are the goals of the Delegatee?

What opportunities exist for the Delegator?

What opportunities exist for the Delegatee?

How, and how often should the Delegatee be monitored?

How, and how often should the Delegatee be encouraged/ motivated?

Who should be evaluated?   How often? By whom?

What problems could arise that would cause the Delegator to need extra patience?

What problems might arise that would cause the Delegatee to need extra patience?

Delegation

Helpful Tools

The Art of Letting Go is not a concrete, rigid process or structure. After all, Delegation is truly an ART – done by different people, in different situations, for different reasons. Just like no two pieces of art are the same, no two delegation arrangements will be same either.

However, rather than having to "start with a blank canvas" each time, the following Helpful Tools have been developed to offer you a framework for creating your next "Masterpiece".

Basic What and Why Delegation Statement

Assignment: _____

Part of the _____ Project

Reason(s) for Delegation:

    1) _____

    2) _____

    3) _____

Benefit to Delegator: _____

_____

Benefit to Delegatee: _____

_____

Benefit to Organization: _____

_____

The LET GO Perspectives

Project: _____

Delegator   Delegatee

Leadership

_____   _____

Empowerment

_____   _____

Training

_____   _____

Goal Oriented

_____   _____

Opportunity

_____   _____

Basic Delegation Ranking Grid

Project: _____

Name	Knowledge	Motivation	Availability	Total

<u>Detailed Delegation Assessment Grid</u>

Name	Job to be Delegated	Skills	Available	Experienced	Willing	Developmental	Oversight level	Motivation style	Evaluation style	Tools needed	Selection Order

Priority Chart

Assignments to be completed:

Project / Assignment	Time required	Due Date	Priority order

** This priority chart can be used for one person or for one multi-component project.

Assignment Chart

As much as we all want to remember who we delegated what to, when, and deadlines, it may not be possible.

Task	Assigned to	Start date	End date	Status Mtg frequency

** This chart can be sorted by Project, by Person, or by Date.

Status Report

Meeting Date: _____   Project: _____

Assigned to: _____   Present at meeting: _____

Goal of project: _____

 Start Date: _____   Projected End Date:_____

Project status as of last meeting (refresh memory)

What was accomplished since last meeting?

- Deliverables?
- Details?
- Reports?
- Info gathered?

What is planned for the upcoming period (week/month/quarter)?

- Deliverables?
- Details?
- Reports?
- Info gathered?

What significant work remains to be done

- 3 weeks/months out?
- 6 weeks/months out?

Are additional info/ tools/resources needed? What? How much? When?

Is project on target for completion?

Date:	On-target	Ahead	Behind
Cost:	On-target	Ahead	Behind

If significantly off track, do we need to re-group, re-work strategy? Why (detail needed)?

Evaluation Form

Date: _____   Project: _____

Evaluation of: _____   My name:_____

My role in project was: Delegator   Delegatee   Other_____

Start Date: _____   End Date:_____

Areas of Recognition (Keep doing these!):

1.

2.

3.

Areas for Improvement (Room to grow):

1.

2.

3.

Overall opinion and comments regarding delegation related to this project:

_____

_____

_____

_____

_____

_____

Delegation

It's time to Let Go!

Now it's time. You've learned what Delegation is, how to do it, and what it takes to be successful.   You've learned the advantages and the barriers. You've been given tools to assist you with your endeavors. Best of all, you've had a chance to get your feet wet by thinking how delegation can work for you, and what each of the components mean to you personally and professionally.   Through the exercises in this book, you've even had a chance to put the skills to work by practicing the techniques. You're ready to Let Go!

Now it's time. Take what you have learned and put it to use. Start RIGHT NOW by jotting down at least 3 things, both personally and professionally, that you will work on delegating. Stretch your imagination if you have to – believe me, the possibilities are endless. When you are done, you can tear out your list and tack it to your wall.

Now it's time to ---- LET GO!

Things I will delegate, on a personal level:

1.

2.

3.

Things I will delegate, on a professional level:

1.

2.

3.

Tips for Successful Delegation

1. Let go – but don't walk away

2. It's about leadership – act and think like a leader

3. It's about training – teach new skills to less experienced members

4. Highlight strengths noted during the project

5. Be respectful of all people in the process

6. Be open to questions and requests for clarification

7. Provide continuous feedback – good and bad

8. Trust your team and yourself

9. There are different ways to do things

10. Perfection is not always necessary (although precision might be)

11. Observe from a distance (no micro-management!)

12. Get to know your team members

13. Delegate up AND down – everyone can help

14. Approach every delegation experience as an opportunity – to learn and to teach

15. Share the results

16. Guide and inspire

17. Break the big projects into pieces

18. Hold periodic status meetings

19. Know your goal – share your goal

20. Have patience – with the project, the team and yourself

Customized Caring, Inc.
www.customizedcaring.com

Amy@customizedcaring.com
630.306.4480

For More Information

Customized Caring, Inc.

901 Indigo Court
Hanover Park, Illinois 60133
www.CustomizedCaring.com

Contact Amy K. Atcha
at
630.306.4480
amy@customizedcaring.com

Life is precious. Take care of those you love.

www.ingramcontent.com/pod-product-compliance
Lightning Source LLC
Chambersburg PA
CBHW080526110426
42742CB00017B/3255